AMAZING ALASKA!

A Raven's Eye View

Deb Vanasse
Illustrated by K.E. Lewis

SASQUATCH BOOKS
SEATTLE

With thanks to John Schauer and all the great teachers of Alaska. C. R. Raven's got nothing on you.

—Deb Vanasse

With gratitude to dear friends and family. Your love and support made this work possible. Thank you!

—K.E. Lewis

Okay, kids. Let's get one thing straight. I'm not a blackbird. Or a crow. The name's Raven. Cornelius Randolf Raven. C. R. for short.

I've got credentials, in case you're wondering. Smart. Sassy. Dumpster savvy. And I never met a roadkill I didn't like.

Forget that sorry excuse for a state bird. Ptarmigan are big on feet and short on brains. Ravens are the real thing. You won't believe the stories they tell about us.

Get ready for a first-class, grade-A, number one tour of the Last Great Place on the earth. We've got a chunk of ground to cover. About 6,000 square miles of it. So let's get moving.

—C. R. Raven

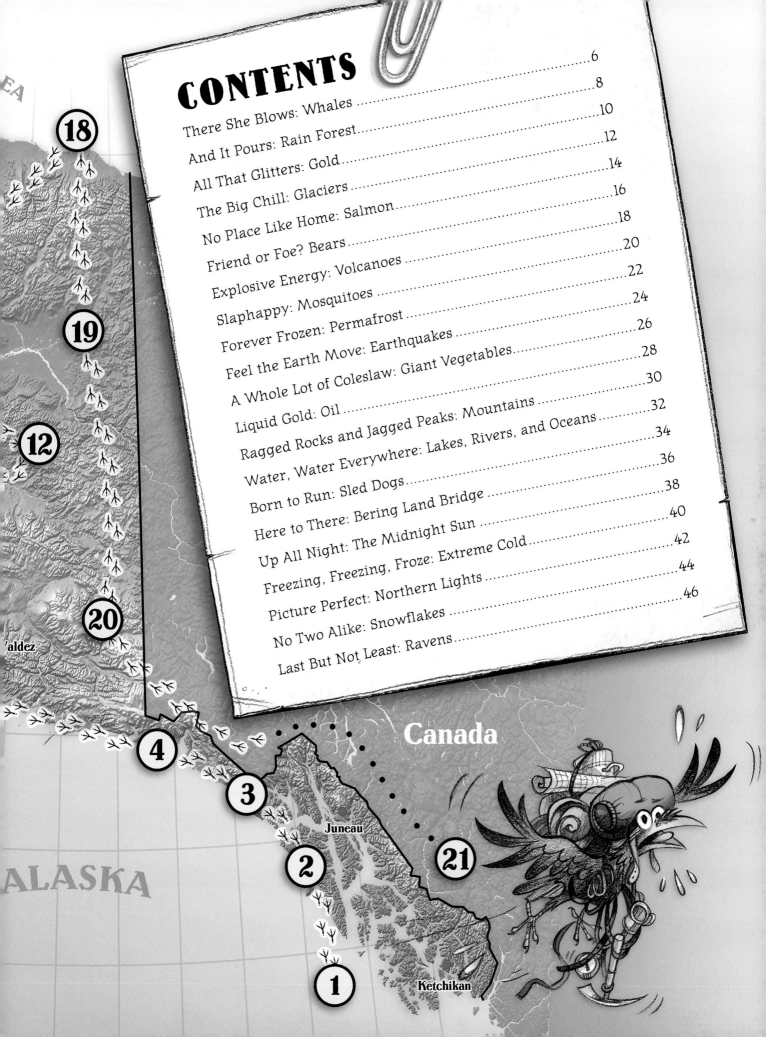

CONTENTS

There She Blows: Whales 6

And It Pours: Rain Forest 8

All That Glitters: Gold 10

The Big Chill: Glaciers 12

No Place Like Home: Salmon 14

Friend or Foe? Bears 16

Explosive Energy: Volcanoes 18

Slaphappy: Mosquitoes 20

Forever Frozen: Permafrost 22

Feel the Earth Move: Earthquakes 24

A Whole Lot of Coleslaw: Giant Vegetables 26

Liquid Gold: Oil 28

Ragged Rocks and Jagged Peaks: Mountains 30

Water, Water Everywhere: Lakes, Rivers, and Oceans 32

Born to Run: Sled Dogs 34

Here to There: Bering Land Bridge 36

Up All Night: The Midnight Sun 38

Freezing, Freezing, Froze: Extreme Cold 40

Picture Perfect: Northern Lights 42

No Two Alike: Snowflakes 44

Last But Not Least: Ravens 46

There She Blows: WHALES

See that big lunker? That there's a whale, spouting off. All sorts of whales cruise the waters around here.

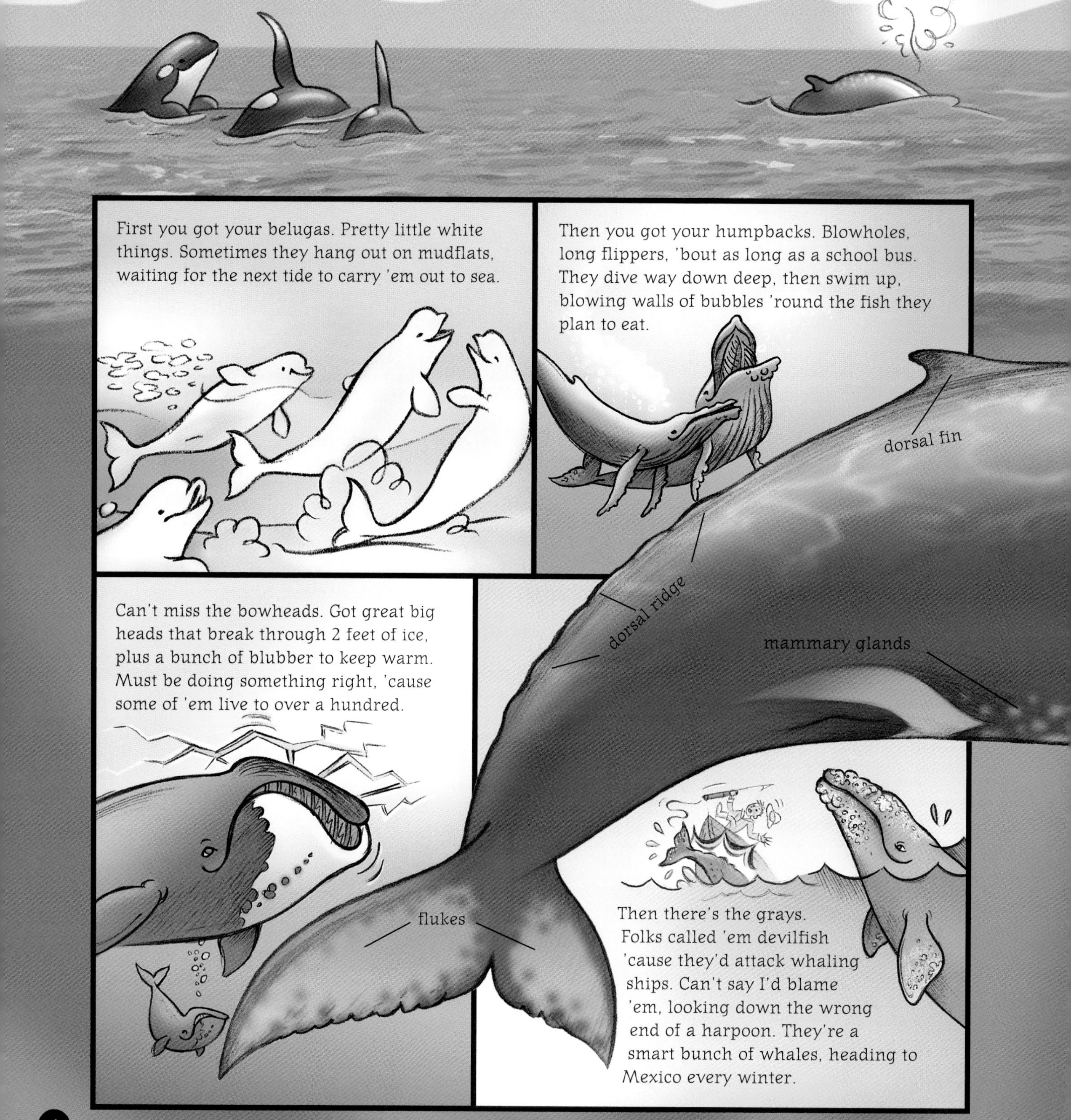

First you got your belugas. Pretty little white things. Sometimes they hang out on mudflats, waiting for the next tide to carry 'em out to sea.

Then you got your humpbacks. Blowholes, long flippers, 'bout as long as a school bus. They dive way down deep, then swim up, blowing walls of bubbles 'round the fish they plan to eat.

dorsal fin

dorsal ridge

mammary glands

Can't miss the bowheads. Got great big heads that break through 2 feet of ice, plus a bunch of blubber to keep warm. Must be doing something right, 'cause some of 'em live to over a hundred.

flukes

Then there's the grays. Folks called 'em devilfish 'cause they'd attack whaling ships. Can't say I'd blame 'em, looking down the wrong end of a harpoon. They're a smart bunch of whales, heading to Mexico every winter.

All whales put on quite a show. Breaching, they jump half out of water and fall back. Spyhopping, they poke their heads up and take a look-see all around. Slapping those flippers and tails on the water, they sure can raise a ruckus. And folks think *I* make a scene.

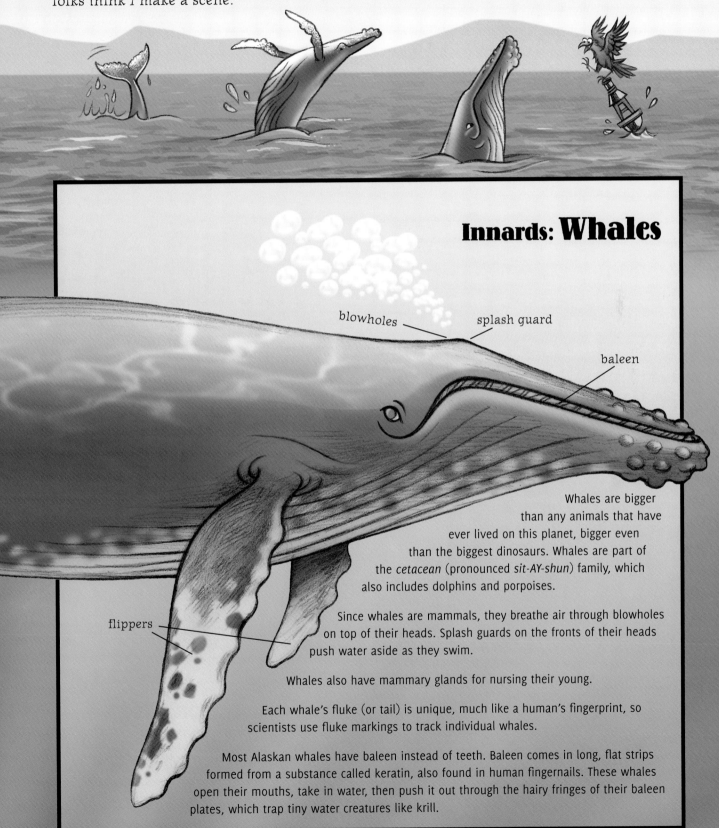

Innards: **Whales**

blowholes   splash guard

baleen

flippers

Whales are bigger than any animals that have ever lived on this planet, bigger even than the biggest dinosaurs. Whales are part of the *cetacean* (pronounced *sit-AY-shun*) family, which also includes dolphins and porpoises.

Since whales are mammals, they breathe air through blowholes on top of their heads. Splash guards on the fronts of their heads push water aside as they swim.

Whales also have mammary glands for nursing their young.

Each whale's fluke (or tail) is unique, much like a human's fingerprint, so scientists use fluke markings to track individual whales.

Most Alaskan whales have baleen instead of teeth. Baleen comes in long, flat strips formed from a substance called keratin, also found in human fingernails. These whales open their mouths, take in water, then push it out through the hairy fringes of their baleen plates, which trap tiny water creatures like krill.

And It Pours: RAIN FOREST

Drip. Drip. Drip. Rains a whole bunch in these parts. As much as 24 inches, depending on where you're at.

Yup, we got ourselves some rain forests right here in Alaska. Some of these trees are hundreds of years old. Rain forests make for great habitat, don't you know. Great big bunch of stuff that's either living or used to be—and even the used-to-be matters, 'cause it turns right around and helps the new life. It's a whole what-you-call ecosystem. Salmon, grizzlies, black bears, river otters, deer, moose, mountain goats, bald eagles, and wolves, not to mention a whole bunch of plants.

And ravens, of course.

northern flying squirrel

Alaska's temperate rain forests stretch in an arc from just below Ketchikan to the Gulf of Alaska.

At 16.8 million acres, the Tongass National Forest is the largest U.S. forest. The Tongass contains 14 percent of the world's rain forest acreage. Alaska's Chugach (pronounced *CHEW-gatch*) National Forest, with 5.6 million acres, also includes some temperate rain forest.

Temperate rain forests get more than 55 inches of rain and snow each year. The average summer temperature is less than 61 degrees Fahrenheit. In these conditions, plants and wildlife thrive.

BIRD'S EYE VIEW: Alaska's Rain Forest

N

Anchorage

Juneau

Chugach National Forest

Tongass National Forest

sitka spruce

8

great gray
owl

bald eagle

red-breasted
sapsucker

moose

sitka black-
tailed deer

river otter

sword fern

devil's club

pine marten

Squawkings: **Nurse Logs**

If you visit a temperate rain forest, you might see nurse logs—and they
have nothing to do with doctors or hospitals. Nurse logs are fallen trees
that offer nourishment to mosses, ferns, and rows of young trees. Roots
of the new trees reach over the logs and down to the ground. When the
nurse logs rot away, the new trees look like they're standing on stilts—
their own roots.

deerberry

meadow
vole

western hemlock

banana slug

lichen

moss

All That Glitters: GOLD

Love those shiny things. Bits of foil. Tinsel off a Christmas tree. Lost earrings. I'm not picky.

But some folks are. GOLD. That's all they want. Plumb crazy about the stuff.

Thing about gold is it's hard to find. And it's a royal pain to get at. But that doesn't stop folks who really want it. Lots of folks 'round these parts caught themselves a bad case of gold fever.

Worst of it happened back in 1898. Couple of boats left Alaska and pulled into the dock at Seattle plumb full of gold.

Pretty soon everybody wanted in on the action. Regular stampede heading north to the Klondike.

Turned out getting rich quick was a lot tougher than it looked. Land route across Canada took two years. Going by boat was the long way around.

Shorter to hop a steamer to Skagway and hike the Chilkoot Trail, but glory be, what a hike that was. Straight uphill most all the way, not to mention going back and forth a few dozen times to fetch your 2,000 pounds of supplies. Meanest 33 miles in history, some said.

Sad thing was, by the time most of those folks got to the Klondike, pert near all the gold was gone. Still, a bunch of folks stayed on, and that's all right by me. More people, more trash.

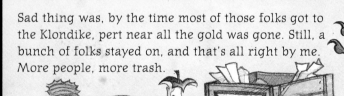

Strut Your Stuff:
Panning for Gold

Want to look for gold? Alaska's a great place to do some panning:

- Find a creek that's open for recreational mining. Nome, Sixmile, Caribou, and Bertha creeks are good spots. Gold panning is also allowed at Hatcher Pass and off the end of the Petersville Road. Avoid private property and posted claims.

- Put on your life jacket, boots, and gloves.

- Fill your pan with sand or gravel from the creek or gravel bars. Don't dig along the vegetated banks, and don't wade out too far into the water.

- Dip your pan to fill it with water.

- Shake back and forth for 2 or 3 minutes.

- Pick out the larger rocks.

- Tilt the pan and let the gravel spill over the side. Add water as needed to keep the mixture soupy. Keep the bottom of the pan lower than the lip so the gold doesn't spill out.

- If you want, use a magnet to pull out the black sand.

- Start using a circular motion as you get to the last of the sand. Hopefully you'll see some color there. Shout out "Bonanza!" when you do.

- Mostly you'll find flakes of gold that gleam instead of glitter. Touch the flakes with your finger. As they stick, rub them from your finger into a container.

What you'll need:
- A small shovel
- A pan with sloping sides
- A small container with a lid
- Rubber boots and gloves
- A life jacket
- An adult
- A magnet (optional)

The Big Chill: GLACIERS

No surprise—it snows a lot up here. And we've got some mighty short summers. So a bunch of that snow never melts. Before you know it, you got yourself a glacier.

Fly up high like I do, and you'll see so many of the dang things you'll lose count. Upwards of a hundred thousand, or so I hear. Can't hardly tell it, but every one of 'em's moving. Backwards, forwards, back again. Can't seem to make up their minds.

But everywhere you turn, they've left their marks. Big old boulders. Piles of gravel. U-shaped valleys. You see all that, you know a glacier's passed on through.

Glaciers sure are pretty. Bright blue hunks of ice tucked up into the mountains. Only blue light rays are strong enough to get through ice that thick.

You can walk right up and touch some of our glaciers, but watch out. Chunks slide off your way, and you're a goner. And up top, there's big old crevasses that'll swallow you up.

Not the friendliest turf for folks like you and me. Darn cold up there, too. I'll skip the slipping and sliding and look from a distance.

Strut Your Stuff: **Ice Worms**

Ice worms are tiny, segmented worms that look like pieces of dark thread. They live only on glaciers, eating the red algae that grows there.

Though tiny, ice worms can hustle, relatively speaking. Using bristles called *setae*, they grip the ice and wiggle along at speeds of up to 10 feet per hour. Scientists are eager to learn how they can survive in near-freezing temperatures.

If you can find a glacier, you can hunt for ice worms.

Rangers at Portage Valley conduct guided Ice Worm Safaris from the Begich, Boggs Visitor Center. Or you can do your own expedition.

Look on blue ice, in slushy snow, and in puddles of glacial melt. Walking on glaciers can be dangerous, so stick to the edges and avoid the faces of glaciers that are known to calve.

Use your shovel to poke around in the snow or icy water. Don't be surprised if you find a lot of ice worms in one spot. They gather in colonies of more than a million.

To get a close look at these little critters, scoop some up with your spoon. Resist the temptation to touch them, as the heat of your hand means instant death to ice worms. They can survive only in the narrow range of 32 to 40 degrees Fahrenheit.

What you'll need:

- A spoon
- A shovel
- A glacier
- An adult

No Place Like Home: SALMON

See that jumble of fish milling around? That there's a bunch of salmon, headed home after a jaunt in the high seas. Looks like nobody told 'em it's mighty tough swimming upstream. They're plumb tuckered out, and none too pretty. Hooked jaws, humped backs, and their shiny silver color's faded clean away.

These fish got themselves an uphill battle pert near from the day they're hatched. When they're just little squirts, the bigger fish try to eat 'em. Then along come your terns and ducks, looking for an easy meal. The lucky ones make it out to the sea, but then they've got to dodge whales, seals, dolphins, and sea lions.

Salmon finally get themselves all grown up and nature starts calling 'em home. So they turn around and head right back to where they came from. Who knows how the darned things find their way. They've got pretty good noses, that's for sure. A single drop of water from their stream mixed up with 250 gallons of seawater, and that's enough to get 'em pointed in the right direction.

Tidbits: Salmon

There are 5 species of salmon in Alaska:

chum
coho
sockeye
chinook
pink

The biggest salmon caught in Alaska weighed 126 pounds.

Salmon will leap obstacles over 12 feet high to get home.

What's the big hurry, you ask? Gotta lay some eggs. About 2 to 14,000, if you can imagine that. Won't lay 'em anywhere except the exact spot where they were hatched themselves. Talk about picky.

TO THE OCEAN

fry

parr

smolt

alevin

roe

Innards: Salmon Life Cycle

Salmon begin life as eggs called *roe*. Roe are laid in a nest called a *redd*. Both male and female Alaskan salmon die after spawning in the same freshwater streams where they were born.

Newly hatched salmon, their yolk sacs still attached, are called *alevin*. The alevin mature into salmon *fry*, which then develop into *parr*. When they reach lengths of 2 to 5 inches, the parr become *smolt* and begin to make their way toward salt water.

After 2 to 7 years in the ocean, salmon return to the freshwater streams where they were hatched to lay their eggs, beginning the cycle again.

15

Friend or Foe?
BEARS

Black bears. Polar bears. Grizzlies. Some folks get plumb scared and others get plain silly around these big bruins. Best way to treat 'em is with a whole lot of respect.

You can tell your polar bears 'cause they're white and they live way up north. From there it gets down-right confusing. You got your brown-colored black bears and your black-colored brown bears, not to mention that there's white brown bears and blue brown bears, too.

Grizzlies? They're nothing but brown bears living real far from the coast. Geesh. Whoever named these guys needs a good talking-to.

Bears get cranky if you sneak up and surprise 'em, so I squawk real loud when I see one coming. Most of the time they mind their own business, which is a good thing. They've got gnarly claws, big teeth, and a whole lot of weight to throw around.

Bears sure know how to eat. They feast on 200,000 berries a day or some such thing. Not that they're picky. Like me, they'll gobble up just about anything, which is why it's a good idea to get your trash out of the way if you're going to tromp around where bears hang out.

Strut Your Stuff: Bear Identification

You can't tell the type of bear by its color, since black and brown bears come in all sorts of color phases. But brown bears have humps between their shoulders. And if you look at one sideways, you can see a dip along its nose, while a black bear has a straight facial profile.

Brown bears also have smaller, more rounded ears than black bears. Their claws are up to 4 inches long, while black bears' claws are rarely more than 2 inches. And if you drew a straight line across the pad of a brown bear track, it wouldn't cross the toes, but the same line would cross a toe or two in a black bear track.

Got it? See if you can tell whether each of the pictures in the orange circles below goes with a black or a brown bear. The answers are at the bottom of the page.

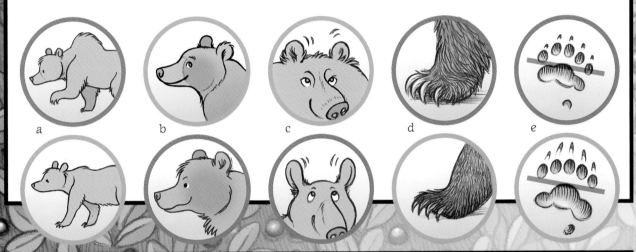

a   b   c   d   e

Tidbits: Bears

More than 98 percent of the brown bears in the United States live in Alaska.

ALASKA OR BUST

At birth, bear cubs weigh less than a pound. They can't see and they're almost bald.

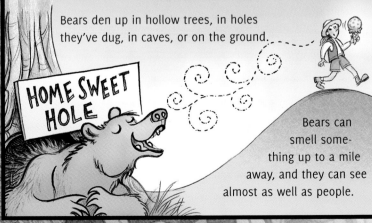

Bears den up in hollow trees, in holes they've dug, in caves, or on the ground.

HOME SWEET HOLE

Bears can smell something up to a mile away, and they can see almost as well as people.

Never try to out-run a bear—they run much faster than people do.

Explosive Energy: VOLCANOES

See those mountains? Might look all quiet and peaceful, but don't let 'em fool you. Those are volcanoes, ready to spit and spew and raise a ruckus.

We've got plenty of potboilers up in these parts. Ring of Fire, that's what they're called. Travel along that tail of islands, the Aleutian Arc, and you're pretty much guaranteed to see a big lid-popper each and every year.

Way back in 1912, Katmai blew for three days. Foot of ash all over Kodiak Island. Big cloud went south and made acid rain. Clothes hanging out got plumb full of holes from the raindrops. Glad I missed that one.

RUSSIA   Alaska   NORTH AMERICA

RING OF FIRE

There are more than 100 volcanoes in Alaska. That's 80 percent of all active volcanoes in the U.S.

Tidbits: Volcanoes

The 1912 Katmai eruption caused a 2-mile-wide crater where the top of the mountain blew off. Scientists predict that at least 10 Alaskan volcanoes are capable of producing an eruption as big as the one at Katmai.

Several thousand people fly over Alaskan volcanoes every day. Because volcanic ash can disable jet engines, flights must sometimes be grounded during eruptions.

Katmai Crater

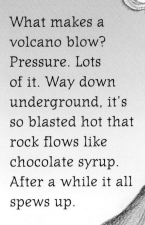

What makes a volcano blow? Pressure. Lots of it. Way down underground, it's so blasted hot that rock flows like chocolate syrup. After a while it all spews up.

Hot lava. Gas. Flying rocks. Big mess. Then come the mudslides. Tsunamis. Earthquakes. Avalanches. And people think *I* cause trouble.

Augustine Volcano

Innards: Mountain Makeover

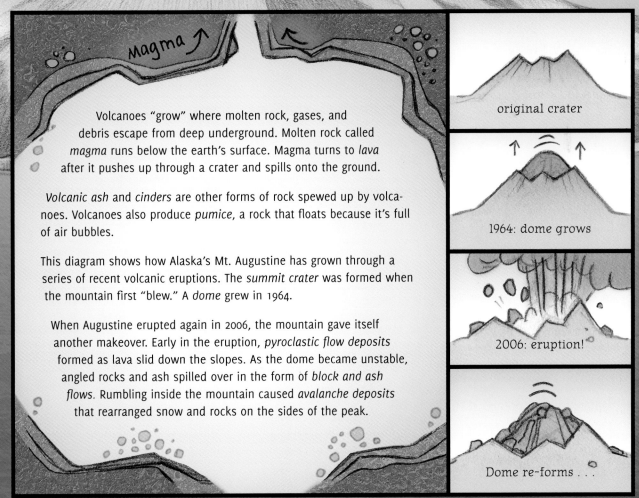

magma ↑

Volcanoes "grow" where molten rock, gases, and debris escape from deep underground. Molten rock called *magma* runs below the earth's surface. Magma turns to *lava* after it pushes up through a crater and spills onto the ground.

Volcanic ash and *cinders* are other forms of rock spewed up by volcanoes. Volcanoes also produce *pumice*, a rock that floats because it's full of air bubbles.

This diagram shows how Alaska's Mt. Augustine has grown through a series of recent volcanic eruptions. The *summit crater* was formed when the mountain first "blew." A *dome* grew in 1964.

When Augustine erupted again in 2006, the mountain gave itself another makeover. Early in the eruption, *pyroclastic flow deposits* formed as lava slid down the slopes. As the dome became unstable, angled rocks and ash spilled over in the form of *block and ash flows*. Rumbling inside the mountain caused *avalanche deposits* that rearranged snow and rocks on the sides of the peak.

original crater

1964: dome grows

2006: eruption!

Dome re-forms . . .

Slaphappy: MOSQUITOES

Bzzzzzzz. The mosquito's not our state bird like some folks think, but they do get attention, the way they poke at folks and suck their blood.

It's not the poke that's so daggone annoying, it's their spit. Mosquito spit makes your blood flow right into the snouts of these little pests, and it makes you itch.

Just don't think you're the only one suffering. Mosquitoes suck blood from animals and birds, and believe you me, there's some places on a bird that are mighty tough to scratch. Some mosquitoes even suck blood from their own kind.

Dang things have been plaguing this earth for 30 million years, and there's about 2,600 species. Thank your stars that only the females want your blood. Need it for laying eggs or some such nonsense.

If you're out in the summertime, hang with a friend. Mosquitoes poke the guy that's warmest, 'specially if he's got more carbon dioxide and lactic acid drifting off his skin. Hopefully that's the other guy.

Tidbits: Mosquitoes

- Alaskan mosquitoes are no bigger than mosquitoes in other places. There are just more of them here. The hordes are thickest north of the Yukon River.
- Although there are more than 2,600 species of mosquitoes in the world, there are probably no more than 25 species in Alaska.
- Females of some species survive the winter, emerging in the spring to lay their eggs.
- In the water stages of their lives, mosquitoes provide an important food source for fish.

Innards: Mosquito Parts and Life Cycle

Mosquitoes are part of the insect order Diptera, which means "True Fly." Like all flies, mosquitoes have two wings, but mosquito wings also have scales.

Hairs on the female's antennae leads her to the blood she needs in order to lay her eggs.

Because they drink nectar instead of blood, males don't have the pointed proboscis.

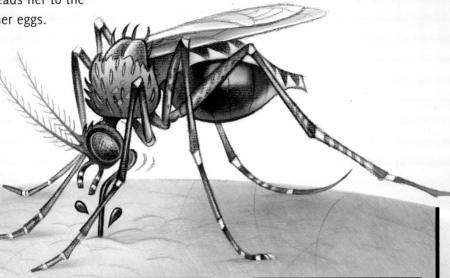

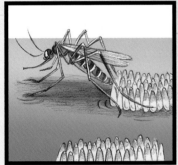

After the female mates and has her blood meal, she lays 40 to 400 eggs, sometimes repeating the cycle several times before she dies.

Mosquito eggs hatch in the water, sometimes after overwintering. Newly hatched mosquitoes take the form of larvae.

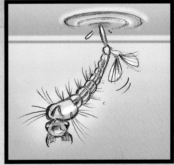

They breathe through tiny tubes that penetrate the water's surface, but they can dive deep when they're disturbed.

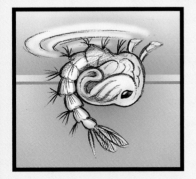

Over several days to weeks, the larvae change to pupae that float on the water.

Each pupa forms a case around itself, emerging in 1 to 4 days as an adult mosquito.

The adult dries its wings and leaves the water to feed and mate, beginning the cycle again.

Forever Frozen: PERMAFROST

Take a look at that dipsy-doodle road. And that kiddy-wampus house. Underneath there's a whole lot you can't see, and it all comes down to ice.

Yup, ice. Permafrost, as folks call it, goes down 1,000 feet deep. Take a gander north of the Brooks Range, and there's nothing but frozen dirt. Continuous, they call it. Farther south, it's spotty. Discontinuous, they say. Hard for stuff to grow in. Top warms in the summer, freezes come winter, and heave-ho, you've got a frost heave. There's your dipsy-doodle road and your kiddy-wampus house.

Permafrost is all over—24 percent of the Northern Hemisphere, if you're counting. That stuff starts to melt, and you've got a heap of troubles. Landslides. Topsy-turvy buildings. Droopy roads. Cracked pipelines. Yikes. Where's the Ice Age when you need it?

BIRD'S EYE VIEW:
Permafrost

North of the Brooks Range, permafrost is continuous—it's everywhere. To the south, it's discontinuous. Stunted trees and wavy roads may indicate frozen soils, but to know for sure, engineers drill core samples.

Continuous

Discontinuous

No permafrost

Strut Your Stuff: Frozen Soils

You can do your own experiment at home to see what happens when soils freeze. After making sure there's room in your freezer:

- Fill 4 paper cups approximately ⅔ full with dirt. Thoroughly wet the dirt and pack it down.

- Insert a Popsicle stick about 2 inches deep in 3 of the cups, packing the soil tight so each stick stands up straight. Label these cups 1, 2, and 3.

- Push a Popsicle stick all the way to the bottom of the fourth cup, being careful not to poke the stick through. Label this cup 4.

- With the marker, draw a line on each stick to mark where it meets the soil.

- Put the cups in the freezer overnight. In the morning, remove the cups. Fill cup 1 to the top with sand or similar material.

- Let all the cups sit for 4 hours at room temperature. Put cup 3 back in the freezer. While cup 3 is in the freezer, study cups 1, 2, and 4. Can you see a difference between the melting in cup 2 as opposed to cups 1 and 4? Cup 2 shows what happens to structures when soil freezes and thaws.

- The next morning, take cup 3 from the freezer. What happened to the stick when you partially thawed the soil and then refroze it? This cup shows how frost heaves occur when thawed soils refreeze.

Sand, as in cup 1, along with gravel and vegetation, has an insulating effect on soils. One method for stabilizing buildings on permafrost is to build a raised foundation on a layer of sand.

Another building method involves driving pilings of steel or treated wood deep into the frozen soils, so deep that summer thawing of the active layer has no effect on the foundation. This is what you've simulated in cup 4.

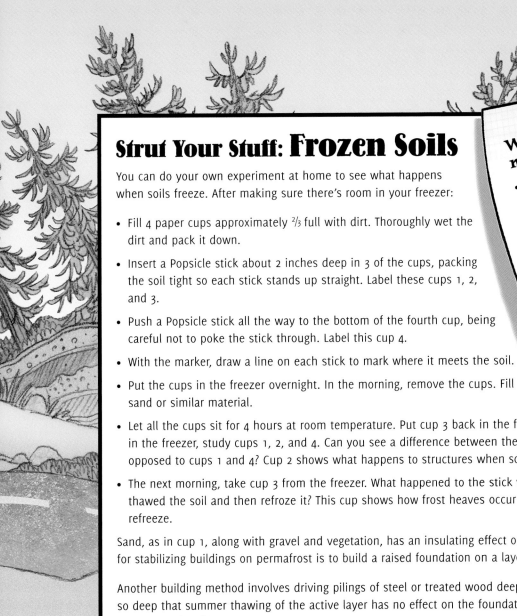

What you'll need:

- 4 paper cups
- 4 Popsicle sticks
- A felt-tipped marker
- Dirt
- Water
- A freezer

Feel the Earth Move:
EARTHQUAKES

Shake, rattle, and roll! That's what happens when the ground gets moving 'round here, and it happens more than you'd think. Average of 13 times a day. That's 6,000 shakers a year.

PLATES

PACIFIC PLATE

Of the world's earthquakes, 11 percent happen right here in Alaska. Sure, some of 'em are puny, but we get some big ones, too. Back in 1964 we had ourselves a 9.2 on a scale of 10. Whole bunch of havoc by the time the dust settled, let me tell you.

So what sets solid ground to shaking? For starters, that stuff under your feet isn't as solid as it looks. Turns out the earth's crust is made of plates, sort of like giant puzzle pieces. And the darned things can't sit still. Crawl along real slow-like, about the same speed as your fingernails grow.

Up here in Alaska, you got your Pacific Plate grinding and diving along your North American Plate, and that's where trouble starts. The edges of those plates slide along like butter, and everybody's happy. But they start jostling around with jagged edges and whatnot, and pretty soon the earth starts a-trembling. Even the ocean gets in on the action, with big old tsunami waves that make for a whole lot of problems.

Turns out you just can't trust the dang dirt. I'll stick to the sky, thank you.

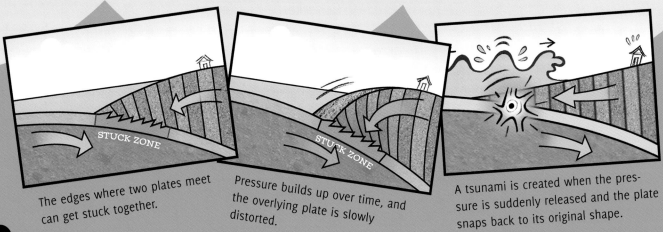

The edges where two plates meet can get stuck together.

Pressure builds up over time, and the overlying plate is slowly distorted.

A tsunami is created when the pressure is suddenly released and the plate snaps back to its original shape.

Squawkings:
The Good Friday Earthquake

On March 28, 1964, the largest earthquake in North America struck the area around Alaska's Prince William Sound. Though the quake lasted only 3 to 5 minutes, it had an incredible impact, damaging 30 blocks of buildings in downtown Anchorage and creating landslides that caused 75 homes to collapse.

Tsunamis triggered by the quake killed 28 people in the town of Valdez, which had to be rebuilt on more stable soils. In the port town of Seward, oil storage tanks erupted into flames, and 12 people died. In all, the quake caused 131 deaths, most of them from tsunamis, and some as far away as California.

Survivors of the quake said it sounded like a freight train roaring past at high speeds. According to scientists, this noise was due to collapsing structures rather than the movement of the earth. Others reported the ground rolling like ocean waves, telephone poles rocking back and forth, and trees whipping down to the ground and then back up again.

In some places, the earth cracked open. In other places, salt water from the tsunami killed acres of forests. The earthquake also caused *seiches*, the sloshing of water in ponds, as far away as Louisiana.

Originally, scientists measured the 1964 earthquake at a magnitude of 8.3 on the Richter scale, but that figure was later revised to 9.2. The energy released in the quake was equal to that of 73,000 atomic bombs. Though earthquakes can't be predicted, scientists are certain that more big shakers are in store for Alaska.

A Whole Lot of Coleslaw:
GIANT VEGETABLES

What's all the fuss about big stuff? I'm not talking mountains, glaciers, or giant brown bears. I'm talking vegetables. Cabbage. Broccoli. Carrots. Zucchini. What do you do with a cabbage that weighs in at pert near 100 pounds?

I know, they look impressive. And they get folks scratching their heads about how we grow 'em so big when our summer's so short. Trick is light. Lots of it. Pushing 20 hours a day come the middle of summer. And cold dirt. Some plants like it chilly.

All this crazy vegetable–growing started way back in the 1930s. Depression was going on, and farmers were hurting for money. So up they came to Alaska, starting a colony in the Matanuska Valley. That's when they found out how big a cabbage could grow in these parts.

Nowadays there's big money for those giant cabbages—5,000 dollars, or some fool thing like that, for the biggest one at the State Fair every year.

That's if the moose don't get 'em first. Far as I'm concerned, the moose can have 'em.

Now a giant French fry, that's a different story.

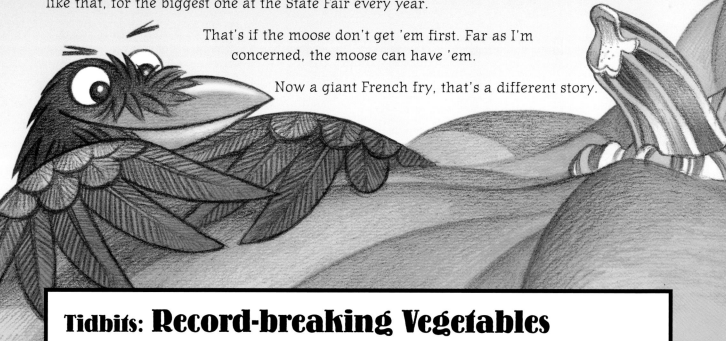

Tidbits: Record-breaking Vegetables

Alaska's giant vegetables have set all kinds of world records. Check out these lunkers:

99-pound cabbage

19.98-pound carrot

59-pound zucchini

35-pound broccoli

Strut Your Stuff:
Plants and Light

You know that plants need light to grow. But is more light better? Find out for yourself.

You may want some friends or classmates to help with this activity:

- Plant 4 seeds in each pot, following the directions on the seed packet. Water thoroughly, measuring to make sure you give each pot the same amount of water. Label the pots as follows: 4 hours, 8 hours, 12 hours, and 24 hours.

- Starting in the morning, set all the pots under the light. Set the timer for 4 hours. When the timer goes off, move the 4-hour pot into the dark. Set the timer for 4 hours again; when it goes off, move the 8-hour pot into the dark. Finally, set the timer for another 4 hours, moving the 12-hour pot into the dark when the timer goes off. Repeat daily. The 24-hour pot stays in the light all the time.

- Keep the soil moist, being careful to water each pot with the same amount of water. Make a chart to record the plants' heights every 5 days. Keep your chart for at least 3 weeks.

What connection did you find between the amount of light and plant growth? Is more light always better?

What you'll need:

- Four 4-inch plant pots with drainage and trays to catch excess water. Disposable pots are fine.
- Soil to fill the pots
- A packet of zucchini or broccoli seeds
- A fluorescent light
- A light-free closet or cupboard
- Labels for each pot
- Water and a measuring cup
- A timer
- A ruler

Liquid Gold: OIL

long-tailed jaeger

There's some thick black goo down there that folks sure do get excited about. Yup, I'm talking oil, running through that big pipeline, 24/7. A couple million barrels of it a day back when things were really flowing. That's a lot of muck.

Way up on the North Slope, you'll find all sorts of drill rigs and such. That's on account of how, millions of years ago, it was all one big ocean.

Along came some mountains pushing that ocean clean out of the way, and before you can say hydrocarbons, you've got critter soup from all the little plants and animals that got buried. Things got pushed down deep and they started cooking. By the time the stuff gets pumped back up, it's pushing 200 degrees.

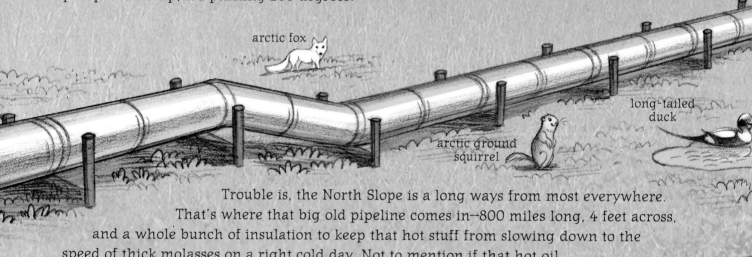

arctic fox

arctic ground squirrel

long-tailed duck

Trouble is, the North Slope is a long ways from most everywhere. That's where that big old pipeline comes in—800 miles long, 4 feet across, and a whole bunch of insulation to keep that hot stuff from slowing down to the speed of thick molasses on a right cold day. Not to mention if that hot oil rubbed up against the permafrost, you'd have a whole heap of trouble on your hands.

pacific loon

Gasoline, diesel, fuel oil, kerosene, wax, even that gol'-darned plastic wrap keeping me from my doughnut—all of it comes from oil. Me, I don't have much use for any of it, 'specially when it's wrapped around that doughnut.

snowy owl

Squawkings: Pipeline Pigs

They don't oink or wallow in the mud, and you can't get bacon out of them, but these mechanical pigs serve a purpose, checking and cleaning the Trans-Alaska Pipeline.

Scraper pigs clean the pipeline to enhance the flow of oil. Corrosion pigs use technology to measure damage to the steel, while deformation pigs detect dents and bends in the pipe.

musk oxen

caribou

spectacled eider

tundra swans

Prudhoe Bay

Fairbanks

Valdez

BIRD'S EYE VIEW:
Trans-Alaska Pipeline

Around 70,000 people helped build the Trans-Alaska pipeline back in 1974. Since then, oil has been flowing at the rate of 5 to 7 miles an hour with very few interruptions.

The entire journey from Prudhoe Bay to Valdez takes about 5 days. Along the way, the pipeline crosses 3 mountain ranges and 34 good-sized streams and rivers.

To appreciate this engineering feat, take a look at these pipeline numbers:

- 554 elevated animal crossings
- 23 buried animal crossings
- 13 pipeline bridges

- 44 road bridges
- 420 miles of pipe above ground
- 380 miles of pipe below ground

rock ptarmigan

caribou

Ragged Rocks and Jagged Peaks:
MOUNTAINS

A bird's got to keep an eye out around these parts. Big rocks jut up every which way you turn. Dang things have been around a while, too. Millions of years ago, big plates of land took to inching their way north. Ended up sort of like a jigsaw puzzle, with mountains pushing up wherever the plates bumped and ground together.

That real tall mountain, that's McKinley. Some folks call it by its Athabaskan name, Denali. Means "high one," which if you ask me is a whole lot better than naming a mountain after some guy who never even saw it.

One mountain, two names, and lots of altitude—20,320 feet of it, to be exact. Daggone thing's so tall it makes its own weather. Lots of times it's all covered in clouds and you wouldn't even know it's there. Folks are plumb crazy about trying to climb it ever since the first fools got to the top back in 1913.

Me, I'll take attitude over altitude any day of the week. That mountain climbing looks like lots of work.

BIRD'S EYE VIEW: Alaska's Many Mountains

More than 20 percent of Alaska's land is over 4,500 feet above sea level.

At 20,320 feet above sea level, Mt. McKinley isn't just the highest peak in Alaska—it's also the second, seventh, and twelfth highest, if you count its south peak (19,470 feet), its South Buttress (15,885 feet), and its East Buttress (14,730 feet). The north peak is the highest in North America. And the mountain is still growing, because the tectonic plates underneath continue to push it upward.

Brooks Range
Ogilvie Mountains
Seward Peninsula Mountains
Yukon-Tanana Uplands
Nulato Hills
Kuskokwim Mountains
Alaska Range
Talkeetna Mountains
Wrangell Mountains
Chugach Mountains
Kenai Mountains
St. Elias Mountains
Aleutian Range
Coast Mountains
▲ Mt. McKinley

Squawkings: **Legends of The Great One**

Alaska's Athabaskan Indians tell this story about Denali. Once, long ago, a man with magical powers, Yako, traveled west to find a wife.

When he came to the village where Totson was chief, one of Totson's wives offered their daughter to be Yako's wife. This angered the chief, who brewed up a furious storm while chasing Yako in his canoe. When Yako used his magic to calm the wind, Totson flung his spear at the younger man.

Sensing danger, Yako turned a huge wave behind him into a wall of rock. The spear ricocheted off the mountain and rocketed into the largest of the waves, which through Yako's magic also turned to stone. Totson's canoe crashed into the newly formed mountain, and Totson was changed into a raven.

Yako made it safely home, where he named the new mountains Denali and Sultana. Today they are officially called Mt. McKinley and Mt. Foraker.

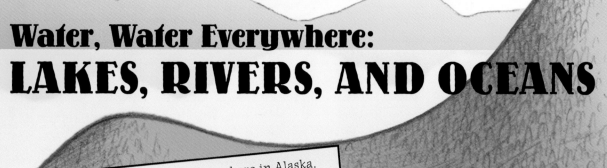

Water, Water Everywhere:
LAKES, RIVERS, AND OCEANS

We've got ourselves a chunk of land up here in Alaska, but we've got a whole lot of water, too—3 million lakes, for starters. Some of them are pretty puny, but I count pert near a hundred that are 10 square miles or more.

And rivers. Whoo ha. We've got 3,000 of those. Maybe you've heard of the Yukon. Longest river in North America, 1,400 miles of it right here in Alaska. Then you've got the Porcupine, the Koyukuk, the Kuskokwim, and the Tanana, each about 500 miles and some change.

Then you've got your salt water. Pacific Ocean, Cook Inlet, Bering Sea, Arctic Ocean. Add up all that shoreline, and it's twice what you've got in the rest of the states. Lots of fishing goes on in those waters, and it can get mighty dangerous when a storm gets to brewing.

Some of our rivers look like they're flowing with milk instead of water. That's from melting glaciers dumping silt. Fish don't like it, but it sure looks pretty.

Me, I'd rather hang out on shore till those boats come and clean up the mess from the fish. Public service, don't you know.

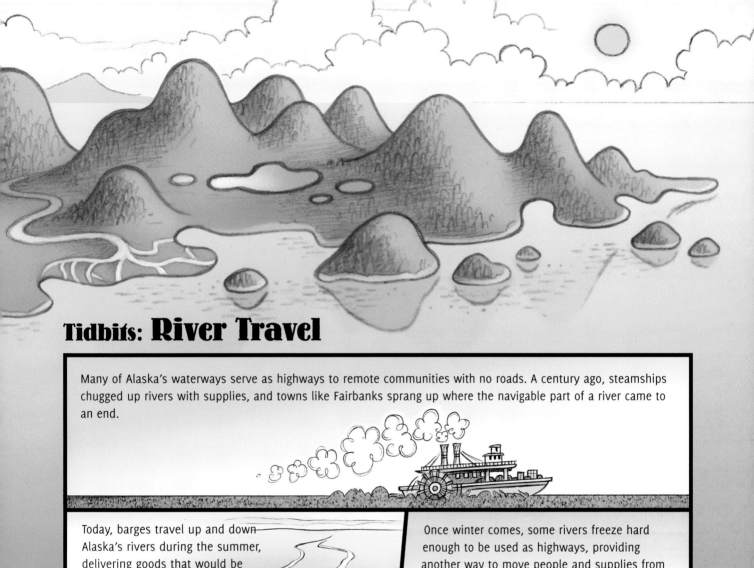

Tidbits: **River Travel**

Many of Alaska's waterways serve as highways to remote communities with no roads. A century ago, steamships chugged up rivers with supplies, and towns like Fairbanks sprang up where the navigable part of a river came to an end.

Today, barges travel up and down Alaska's rivers during the summer, delivering goods that would be too expensive to ship by air.

Once winter comes, some rivers freeze hard enough to be used as highways, providing another way to move people and supplies from one village to another.

Alaskans have a lot of fun on their rivers. Whitewater rafting is a popular way to see some of the state's scenic spots. Rivers are ranked in classes from I through V, with five being the roughest and most treacherous:

Class I: Small waves; passages clear; no serious obstacles.

Class II: Bigger waves; tougher rapids; passages mostly clear.

Class III: Lots of waves; big rocks; eddies; rapids with narrow passages.

Class IV: Powerful waves; lots of rapids; dangerous rocks; swirling eddies; precise maneuvering required.

Class V: Long, violent rapids, almost without interruption; obstructed riverbeds; steep drops; violent currents.

Born to Run: SLED DOGS

Yip. Yap. Howl. All sorts of dogs, all waiting their turn.
Not for their chow, mind you, but for a chance to get hooked up
to a sled and run like the dickens.

There's proof that folks up north were using sled dogs to pull their loads way back 1,000
years ago. Nowadays, sled dogs mostly run in races.

First weekend in March, just like clockwork, dogs get their tails a-wagging and their feet
a-trotting in the Iditarod Sled Dog Race, from Wasilla all the way to Nome. Dozens of
teams, 12 to 16 dogs in each. Snow, wind, cold. Pert near 1,200 miles of it. Sounds crazy, but
folks love it, and the dogs do, too.

Those dogs and mushers get the racing fever. Don't take much time
off, even in the summer. Mushers hook their teams to sleds on wheels
and away they go. Summer,
winter. Run, pull. Not my idea
of fun, but it sure is theirs.

Innards: Anatomy of a Sled Dog

Sled dogs, often called Alaskan Huskies, are a mix of breeds that love to run and pull. Usually they weigh less
than 55 pounds, but they're strong for their size.

Most Alaskan Huskies have long legs, deep, slim chests, heavy fur undercoats, and large thigh muscles. Often
their tails are curved. Their eyes may be brown or blue, or they may have one of each color, as Siberian Huskies
sometimes do.

While normal dogs eat around 1,500 calories per day, racing dogs need closer to 10,000. And though they're bred
to be strong and fast, these dogs have sensitive feet. In a 10-day race like the Iditarod, a musher may go through more
than 2,000 polar fleece booties for a single dog team.

Squawkings: Balto

One of the most famous sled dogs of all time is Balto, who led a team of dogs through a raging blizzard to save the children of Nome.

When deadly diptheria broke out in the remote gold rush town in January 1925, doctors knew they needed serum quickly, or many lives would be lost.

But the only airplane in Alaska had been dismantled for winter, so 20 mushers gathered their teams and set out to run 660 miles in relays to deliver the serum.

The dogs ran through brutal temperatures rarely warmer than 40 degrees below zero. In places, the wind was so strong that it toppled dogs and sleds. Rough ice marred the trail.

Toward the end of the relay, Balto's team encountered a blizzard so fierce that the musher, Gunner Kaasen, sometimes couldn't see his own dogs.

Balto managed to find and keep the trail, delivering the serum to Nome just six days after the run began.

Balto was proclaimed a hero. For the next two years he toured the country. Today, a statue of him stands in New York's Central Park, and the modern Iditarod Sled Dog Race commemorates the famous serum run to Nome.

Here to There:
BERING LAND BRIDGE

Funny thing, getting from here to there. Got a pair of wings like I do, you can get to pretty much wherever you want, no big deal. But those critters that depend on their legs, that's a different story.

ALASKA Now Open!

Lucky for them, things were easier back around 14,000 years ago when ice covered a good chunk of the world. With a whole bunch of water locked up in ice, the oceans were 360 feet lower than they are today.

That made for some dry land where there was none before. Sure as you can say *tromp those tootsies*, herds of critters like mammoth, mastodon, and bison just had to check out a brand-new patch that opened up between where Alaska and Russia are today. Migrated clean across and spread all over.

Right on their tails were a bunch of people, and they spread out, too. That land they crossed, it's called Beringia.

About 8,000 years ago, lots of ice melted clean away and water spread over Beringia. Now it's 800 feet under the Bering Sea. That's why a bird like me prefers the air. It stays right where you left it.

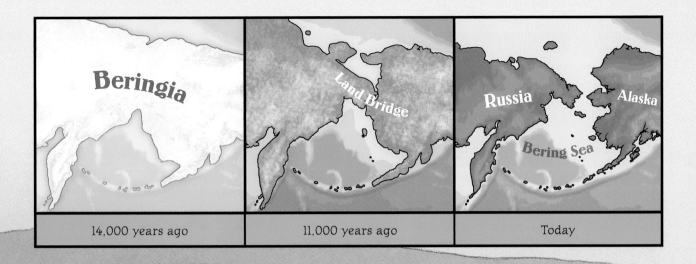

Beringia	Land Bridge	Russia / Alaska / Bering Sea
14,000 years ago	11,000 years ago	Today

Squawkings: A Mystery Unfolds

How did the first people end up in North and South America? Not everyone agrees. Scientists studying anthropological, archaeological, and linguistic data believe that the first Americans migrated from other places. But how they got there is still up for debate.

In 1932, archaeologists found human artifacts dating back to 11,200 BCE near Clovis, New Mexico. The find suggested that people crossed the Beringia land bridge about 12,000 years ago and spread south.

But not all scientists agreed with the "Clovis Theory." Some thought that Beringia would have been tough to cross on foot. Others questioned whether people could have migrated past the ice in Canada. Still others believed that at least some of the humans in the New World first arrived by boat.

In 1997, archaeologists announced a find that shook the Clovis Theory to its core. In southern Chile, a site with remains of dwellings, tools, and preserved plants turned out to be 12,500 years old. If the Clovis people had only reached New Mexico 11,200 years ago, how could scientists explain a site so far to the south some 1,300 years *earlier*?

At this point, no one is sure how people first came to the Americas. There may have been several waves of inhabitants who came from different places in different ways, including travel by boat. Scientists admit that what once seemed certain is in fact still a mystery, and only with further study will we learn the truth.

Up All Night:
THE MIDNIGHT SUN

Long, long days. Long, long nights. We've got it all up here. Course we love those long summer days. Makes a bird feel all warm and peppy inside. Sun's still shining even at midnight, so there's plenty of time for strutting and squawking and scavenging.

Why the long days? Turns out the world doesn't stand up quite straight. Come June 21st, the North Pole's tilted toward the sun, and before you can say *nonstop daylight*, you've got yourself a midnight sun.

Folks up here don't miss a chance to have fun, so on the 21st there's all sorts of whooping and hollering and staying up all night. Suits me just fine. All that merrymaking means all sorts of food, and naturally a bunch of it gets left lying around. That's cause for celebrating, all right.

BIRD'S EYE VIEW: Midnight Sun

As the earth revolves around the sun, its axis is tilted 23.5 degrees. When the top of the axis points away from the sun, it's winter in the Northern Hemisphere. Above the Arctic Circle, the sun doesn't shine for several weeks, creating the effect of one long night. In Barrow, Alaska, the sun sets in mid-November and doesn't come up until the end of January.

Then the earth circles around to where its axis points to the sun. In Barrow, the sun rises in May and doesn't set until early August, creating the impression of an endless day.

summer   spring   23.5 degree tilt   fall   winter

38

Strut Your Stuff: Midnight Sun

You can simulate the effect of the seasons on the amount of daylight by trying this simple demonstration.

In this demonstration, the orange represents the earth, the lamp represents the sun, and the white pin represents the North Pole.

- With the help of an adult, press the white pin into the top of the orange. Using the protractor, measure 23 degrees from the white pin and insert the red pin. Tilt the orange so that the red pin is at the top and the white pin is off to one side.

- Ask the adult to remove the lampshade, turn on the lamp, and hold one end of the yardstick at the base of the lamp. Position the lamp so that you can hold the other end of the yardstick next to the orange.

- Dim the lights and walk a slow circle around the lamp, holding your end of the yardstick to the orange while the adult holds the other end at the base of the lamp. Hold the orange steady against the yardstick, with the red pin pointing straight up.

- Stop when the white pin is beyond the light of the lamp. This would be arctic winter, when the sun doesn't rise. Stop again when the white pin is in the light. This is arctic summer, when the sun doesn't set.

39

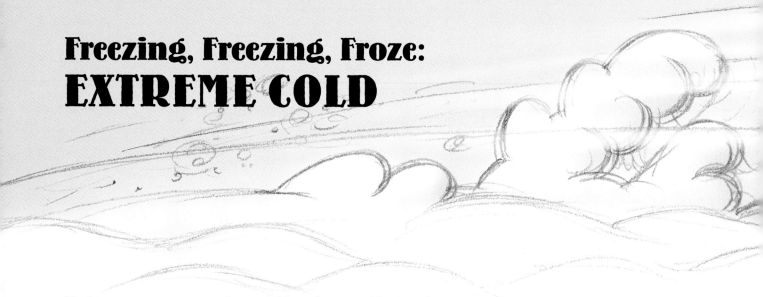

Freezing, Freezing, Froze:
EXTREME COLD

No big surprise—it gets dang cold up here in Alaska. Come the middle of winter, that old thermometer drops to 30, 40, even 50 below zero. Yup, that's chilly. But we all keep going. Schools pert near never close, and kids bundle up for recess down to 20 below.

One time at Alaska's Prospect Creek Camp, back in 1971, the temperature plunged to 80 below. Brrrrrrr and double brrrrrrr.

Toss in a good stiff winter wind, and boy, do you have something to shiver about. So, 30 below with a 30-mile-per-hour wind feels like 67 below, 'cause the wind pulls the heat right off your skin. That's where a bird's mighty grateful for some feathers.

Tidbits: 40 Below

All sorts of unusual things happen at 40 degrees below zero:

Soap bubbles will shatter instead of pop.

Hot water tossed from a cup into the air will disappear, evaporating before it hits the ground.

Water poured on metal will crackle as it freezes.

Water vapor from car exhaust, power plants, and exhaled breath turns to ice, creating a thick fog called ice fog.

Squawkings: How Critters Cope with Extreme Cold

When you live somewhere as cold as Alaska, you do your best to adapt. For humans, that means building super-insulated houses and wearing the best cold-weather gear they can find.

Arctic animals have all sorts of unique ways of surviving the extreme cold. Some insects are freeze-tolerant. As a darkling beetle's temperature drops, water seeps out of its cells. That way, the beetle can withstand temperatures down to 76 below. Other beetles avoid freezing by producing antifreeze that allows them to survive even lower temperatures.

Other animals hibernate to get through the long, icy winter. The body temperatures of bears drop about 10 degrees when they're in hibernation mode, while the body temperatures of hibernating arctic squirrels actually drop below freezing.

By studying hibernation in these animals, scientists hope to make discoveries that will help humans in hospitals and even in space.

Picture Perfect: NORTHERN LIGHTS

Sure are some pretty sights up here. Take those northern lights. Aurora borealis, if you want to get technical.

There you are, staring at a big black sky, and all of a sudden there's light fluttering and prancing all around. Not even us ravens can dance like that.

Believe it or not, these wild things come from the sun. It spits out charged particles, and Earth's got a magnetic field. Put those together, toss in gases way up high, and you get some of the nicest colors you ever did see. Pinks, greens, whites, purples, and reds, all shimmering and bouncing around in the sky.

Wish I could get a better look, but from what I hear, the darned things never get closer than 60 miles to the ground. That'd be quite a trip for an old bird like me.

Tidbits: Aurora Facts

- The aurora appears as ribbons of light that twist and fold in on themselves. It may also appear as a shimmering, dancing curtain.

- Solar winds blast particles from the sun all the way to the edges of the solar system. As these particles are drawn to Earth's magnetic poles, they collide with gases, creating the colors of the aurora.

Tonight, expect clear skies and an ACTIVE aurora borealis...

WEATHER

- While Alaskan communities like Talkeetna, Fairbanks, and Fort Yukon enjoy great aurora viewing now, the North Pole is shifting west. So in 50 to 100 years, aurora viewing opportunities will shift westward.

- Because the sun's most intense energy comes from coronal holes that develop a few years after heavy sunspot activity, scientists can predict auroras with some accuracy. Some Alaskan newspapers feature aurora forecasts alongside weather reports.

Squawkings: Shows in the Sky

For centuries, people have gazed at the northern lights and wondered what they were. According to some Yup'ik and Inupiat legends, the aurora shines through a path where spirit people take the dead.

Some say whistling will make the aurora come close, while others say it will make it go away.

In medieval Europe, the red aurora was believed to be a bad omen, signifying blood and battle.

Uh oh...

Scientists originally thought that the aurora was caused by light reflecting off ice crystals. But in 1934, Sydney Chapman noted that the colors of the aurora differed from the colors in the reflective light of rainbows and prisms. He proposed that solar gases interacted with the earth's magnetic field to produce these spectacular displays.

Today, scientists use magnetometers, all-sky cameras, photometers, radar, rockets, and satellites to study the aurora. Auroras have been observed on other planets, too, including Jupiter, Saturn, and Uranus.

No Two Alike: SNOWFLAKES

You live around here, you're gonna see some snow. In some places, the snow starts falling in September and doesn't quit 'til May. Folks might not like the slippery roads and the walks that need shoveling, but snow is pretty incredible stuff.

All that snow, all those snowflakes. Some look like little stop signs. Some look like needles. Some look like lacy stars. Some form big clumps that flutter down like feathers.

Pert near every snowflake starts around a little bit of dust or some such thing. From there it's the temperature and moisture and what they go bumping into on the way down that gives each one its very own shape.

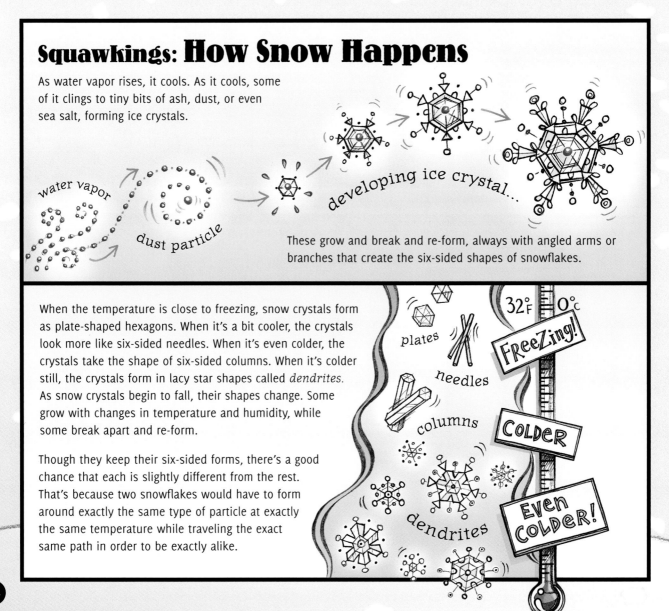

Squawkings: How Snow Happens

As water vapor rises, it cools. As it cools, some of it clings to tiny bits of ash, dust, or even sea salt, forming ice crystals.

water vapor

dust particle

developing ice crystal...

These grow and break and re-form, always with angled arms or branches that create the six-sided shapes of snowflakes.

When the temperature is close to freezing, snow crystals form as plate-shaped hexagons. When it's a bit cooler, the crystals look more like six-sided needles. When it's even colder, the crystals take the shape of six-sided columns. When it's colder still, the crystals form in lacy star shapes called *dendrites.* As snow crystals begin to fall, their shapes change. Some grow with changes in temperature and humidity, while some break apart and re-form.

Though they keep their six-sided forms, there's a good chance that each is slightly different from the rest. That's because two snowflakes would have to form around exactly the same type of particle at exactly the same temperature while traveling the exact same path in order to be exactly alike.

plates

needles

columns

dendrites

32°F 0°C

FREEZING!

COLDER

EVEN COLDER!

There's a whole lot of air trapped between fallen snowflakes, and that helps keep a body warm. Snow makes for good shelter if you get stuck out in the cold, but don't be looking for a bunch of igloos in Alaska. No more igloos than raven castles 'round these parts.

Tidbits: Snow

While most snowflakes are less than 1 inch across, flakes up to 2 inches wide may form in near-freezing temperatures.

Air holds more water vapor at warm temperatures; heaviest snowfalls occur when it's 15 degrees or warmer near the ground.

When the snow is deep, its temperature is warmer closer to the ground, because snow is such a good insulator.

The Inuit people of Canada and Greenland used igloos more than the Inupiat and Yup'ik people of Alaska did.

The colder the snow, the more it crunches and creaks when you walk on it.

Fresh, fluffy snow absorbs sound, while icy, hard-packed snow reflects it.

Last But Not Least: RAVENS

Seems like we just got started, and here it is, the end of the road. It's been quite a trip. But there's something we haven't covered, and that's us ravens. Folks think we're just about dumpster diving and scavenging and such. It's time to set the record straight.

Sure, we can work a dumpster. Nothing better than day-old doughnuts and Chinese takeout. But, hey, we're cleaning up the messes other folks left behind. Think of the trash there'd be if it weren't for us.

Thing about us ravens is we're real Alaskans. None of this flying south when the going gets tough. When it's 40 below, we're still hopping.

And we're smart. Not bragging, just a fact. Hide some food, and chances are we'll find it. Toss us a couple doughnuts, and we'll figure out how to carry both in a single trip.

Tidbits: Ravens

- Ravens like to play in updrafts of wind near cliffs or tall buildings.
- Ravens eat just about anything people do, as well as a lot of spoiled food and garbage that would make people sick.
- Ravens will appear within minutes to "share" what a wolf pack has killed. Some scientists think that wolves hunt in packs so there are more of them to chase off ravens.
  - Many of ravens' dramatic displays, including fluffing out their feathers and aerobatics, are part of their courtship rituals.
  - Ravens make dozens of different sounds, including cackles, caws, and squawks. They can also mimic what they hear.

Plus we're some of the best acrobats around. Swooping, barrel rolling, diving—you name it. We'll grab a branch and swing upside down. Or we'll drop a stick in midair, then catch it again. Try that, you feather-footed state birds.

So forget those ptarmigan, and look me up next time you're up this way. I'll be around.

—C. R. Raven

Squawkings: Raven Tales

In Alaskan native lore, Raven appears as a trickster, a creator, and a transformer. Among the Tlingit and the Haida, the raven is one of several clan crests. Carved on totem poles, Raven sometimes sits beside the sun or atop a wooden box, as represented in one of several stories of how he brought light to the world.

According to legend, Raven created much of what we see on earth, but the world was dark because an old chief kept the sun in a box. Raven tricked the chief by transforming himself into a noisy, whiny child.

The old man finally gave in to the child's demands and handed him the box. Raven opened it, changed himself back to a bird, and flew away with the sun.

As some tell it, Eagle tried to steal the sun from Raven. When they wrestled for it, bits of light fell away, creating the moon and the stars. In the end, Raven placed the sun in the sky, and the world had light.

Manufactured in China in January 2010 by C&C Offset Printing Co. Ltd. Shenzhen, Guangdong Province
Published by Sasquatch Books
Distributed by PGW/Perseus
15 14 13 12 11 10   9 8 7 6 5 4 3 2 1

Cover design: K.E. Lewis
Interior design: Rosebud Eustace
Editor: Michelle Roehm McCann

Library of Congress Cataloging-in-Publication Data

Vanasse, Deb
Amazing Alaska: a raven's eye view / Deb Vanasse; illustrated by K.E. Lewis.
   p. cm.
ISBN 978-1-57061-542-9
1. Alaska--Juvenile literature. I. Lewis, K.E., ill. II. Title
F904.3 .V36
979.8--dc22   2009039490

Page 25 left: Courtesy of the U.S. Geological Survey Photographic Library
Page 25 right: Courtesy of the National Oceanic and Atmospheric Administration (Central Library)
Page 45: Snowflake images courtesy of Kenneth Libbrecht—www.snowcrystals.com

Sasquatch Books
119 South Main Street, Suite 400
Seattle, WA 98104
(206) 467-4300
www.sasquatchbooks.com
custserv@sasquatchbooks.com

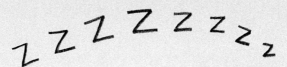